LINE OF SIGHT

WORK *with* LORD PENTLAND

LINE OF SIGHT

WORK *with* LORD PENTLAND

Barbara Probst

CODHILL
PRESS

Codhill Press books
are published for David Appelbaum

First Edition
Printed in the United States of America

front cover photograph: © 1982 David Sailors
photograph post-production: Luis Morales

cover and interior design: Alicia Fox
www.afoxcreativestudio.com

ISBN 978-1-949933-14-7

Lord John Pentland cared above all else about the Gurdjieff work. The material in this book shows the many ways in which he followed this in everything he did.

These reflections from Barbara Probst's years as Lord Pentland's secretary are a unique and valuable example of how Lord Pentland brought alive many, many subtleties of the Gurdjieff teaching into daily life.

—Mary S. Rothenberg

INTRODUCTION

A number of months after Lord Pentland's death in February of 1984, I met with Mary Rothenberg, his daughter, at a small park on the corner of Sixty-Sixth Street and Third Avenue in Manhattan, a block from the building where Lord Pentland had lived. As his executor, Mary had a check to give me.

In Lord Pentland's will, there was a small bequest to "The Secretary." I wasn't mentioned by name. No one was. It was a gift to whoever happened to be in that role when he died.

The wording of Lord Pentland's bequest was significant. There was a position called "secretary" that others had occupied before me; I was merely the last in the chain. Had he lived another five or ten years, Mary would have been handing the check to someone else.

The moment in the little park comes back to me as I prepare this manuscript, which relates events that took place during the years I served as Lord Pentland's secretary. Because of that position, I had the good fortune to witness a little-known aspect of his life.

Many people knew Lord Pentland from activities at the Gurdjieff Foundation; some spent time with him in the summer, traveled with him, cooked for him. Few, however, knew him as a businessman working in his Madison Avenue office, and many—especially those who have come to the Gurdjieff Work in recent decades—may be unaware that he went to the office nearly every day he was in New York, including the day he died. Entrusted by Gurdjieff to lead the Work in America and head of The Gurdjieff Foundation from its establishment in 1953 until his death, Lord Pentland nonetheless placed great importance on being *in life,* fully and productively engaged in a range of endeavors.

Knowing how tricky even the best memory can be and afraid that mine would, over time, begin to distort and omit, I wrote down my recollections several years after his death and shared them with a few people who had known him well. It seemed important—my concluding task as his secretary—to preserve this side of his life, especially as he practiced it in his final years. It was never my intention to circulate the material outside that small radius, and certainly not to make it public.

But times change. Accounts of his influence are starting to emerge, prompting a reassessment of whether I have the right to withhold this unique material. Unlike some accounts, however, this is not a memoir. That is, it is not the story of a personal journey, but a collection of impressions that I received while serving as Lord Pentland's secretary.

In editing and expanding my notes for publication, I've tried to refrain from projection and interpretation—that is, from attributing a specific intention to what Lord Pentland said or did. Rather, I've attempted to stay close to what the experiences brought me, personally.

Even so, the danger in writing about someone above one's own level of being, like Lord Pentland, is always that of reduction. I'm writing, of necessity, from my own level of understanding, which can only provide a partial reflection of what may have actually occurred. Nonetheless, if Lord Pentland's example can provide guidance on how to bring Gurdjieff's teaching into one's daily life, it may be a risk worth taking.

ABOUT G.I. GURDJIEFF

For those unfamiliar with the teaching of G.I. Gurdjieff or the Foundation established to carry out his work, an introductory note may be useful.

George Ivanovich Gurdjieff (1866–1949) was a philosopher, mystic, spiritual teacher, writer, and composer of Greek and Armenian descent. His system of human development has a deep resonance with many ancient teachings—from the esoteric Christianity of the Desert Fathers to Buddhist, Sufi, and other traditions that have since been lost. However, it is unique in its comprehensiveness, spanning levels of existence from cosmology to psychology, and its adaptability to diverse conditions of life.

This adaptability is evident in Gurdjieff's history of teaching in different ways at different times—leading his early pupils across the Caucasus Mountains during the Russian Revolution, converting the former Château Le Prieuré into a residential Institute, hosting elaborate feasts at his apartment in Paris during the German occupation. He also made several trips to America while working on a series of books that were published after his death.

Gurdjieff's system of thought rests on the premise that human beings do not possess a unified consciousness and thus live their lives in a state of "waking sleep," but that it is possible to awaken to higher states of consciousness through a serious, sincere, and multi-faceted "work on oneself." This work on oneself—addressing mind, body, and feelings—can be carried out in the midst of regular life, without having to retreat to a monastery or ashram.

At the same time, many of the practices that Gurdjieff developed lie outside the activities of ordinary life and need to be carried out under specific conditions. These include sacred dances or "Movements," sitting meditations, and group meetings where "students regularly come together to participate in a collective atmosphere that is meant to function as a principal means for the transformation of the individual state of consciousness. Although, with the help of more advanced pupils, questions are shared and responded to in words, the fundamental support of the group is directed to the individual work of facing oneself..." (From the Introduction to *The Inner Journey: Views from the Gurdjieff Work*, Morning Light Press, 2008, ed. Jacob Needleman. Needleman's seventeen-page introduction provides a good overview of Gurdjieff's biography, writings, and fundamental ideas.)

Gurdjieff's teaching thus has two aspects: activities that take place at special centers, known as "Foundations," and practices or exercises that can be carried out in the course of one's daily life.

To those who knew him, Lord Pentland was an exemplar of both. As president of the Gurdjieff Foundation, he led weekly groups, presided over forums, and oversaw special weekend and summer activities. He also brought Gurdjieff's teaching into every part of his "regular" life—including his business office at 790 Madison Avenue.

ABOUT LORD PENTLAND

Lord John Pentland (1907–1984) was a businessman and member of the British House of Lords who spent much of his career conducting government and commercial affairs with the United States, while also serving as president of the Gurdjieff Foundation in America.

Born Henry John Sinclair, Lord Pentland was knighted in December of 1924 at the age of eighteen, upon the death of his father, the first Baron Pentland. His father, a liberal politician, served as Secretary for Scotland from 1905 to 1912, and as Governor General of the Indian state of Madras from 1912 to 1919. Lord Pentland thus spent a portion of his boyhood in India.

Lord Pentland was admitted to Trinity College, Cambridge, and graduated with a Master's degree in 1929, qualifying as a civil engineer. He worked for several British companies over the next decade, rising to the level of director, and in 1944 was appointed to the Combined Production and Resources Board—a cooperative effort of the United States, France, and England, headquartered in Washington D.C.

During this same period, Lord Pentland also became a pupil of P.D. and Mme. Ouspensky, early students of Gurdjieff who had broken with their teacher in the 1920s to continue on their own.

When Ouspensky died in 1947, Lord Pentland's life took a profound turn. As Walter Driscoll quotes in *Transmission: an interview with Lord Pentland*:

> When I met Gurdjieff, I'd been quite a few years with Mr. Ouspensky and Mme. Ouspensky attending talks and lectures and also living in Mme. Ouspensky's house, in their houses in England in the west of London and in New Jersey. And it was after Ouspensky died and I went out to India, and on the way back, actually, it became clear to me that even all those years with Ouspensky, I hadn't arrived at anything; I came to nothing. And it was then that through Mme. Ouspensky's introduction, I went to Paris and met Gurdjieff. I was with him in Paris and then I came to New York. And it was a short period, only about nine months, but a couple of months after that he died. And the way he left things, it made it perfectly easy for me to have to really enter into a position of responsibility as such.

Lord Pentland settled in New York to lead the Work in America and became a permanent resident in the early 1950s. In 1954, he founded his own company, the American British Electric Corporation, and served as its president until his retirement in 1979.

It is striking, but perhaps not surprising, that Lord Pentland's career as president of American British Electric began at the same time as his tenure as president of the Gurdjieff Foundation. He became head of the New York Foundation upon its inception in 1953, and of the Gurdjieff Foundation of California which he established two years later. He held both positions until his death and was instrumental in spreading the Gurdjieff Work throughout the United States.

Lord Pentland was also executive editor of Far West Editions and founder of the Far West Institute, which hosted a series of public lectures in San Francisco between 1974 and 1984 that engaged a wide range of prominent speakers, from various vocations and traditions, in penetrating dialogues about their search for meaning in the midst of contemporary life.

CONTENTS

790 Madison Avenue, Suite 405

As noted, Lord Pentland was a businessman who formed his own company, the American British Electric Corporation, when he established permanent residency in the United States. American British served as a kind of middleman, helping British firms obtain contracts for resource development projects, bridge and tunnel construction, land surveys, geophysical exploration, and similar endeavors. When I asked him how he had come to that profession, Lord Pentland told me that he'd wanted to find a line of work that "did no harm."

Although American British had many clients over the years, by the time I arrived in 1978 nearly all its work was as the representative for a British firm called Hunting Surveys and Consultants. The "staff" consisted of Lord Pentland, the president; a secretary; and Dick Brower, who oversaw contracts for Hunting with the United Nations, the World Bank, and American oil companies.

In early 1979, Lord Pentland negotiated a new arrangement in which Hunting took over the New York office, providing a monthly stipend to cover rent, salaries, and other expenses. Though officially retiring from his role as Hunting's American director—as part of the agreement, and in appreciation for his years of service—Lord

Pentland was permitted to use the office for other business as long as it didn't conflict with Hunting's interests. Thus, he continued to come to work every day, although his work now centered on other projects—films and books about Gurdjieff's teaching, relations with groups in other countries, and his own writing.

Lord Pentland had moved from his former office at Rockefeller Plaza before my arrival. He told me he'd had his eye on the 790 Madison Avenue building because it was the right size—four stories—and walking distance from both his apartment and the Gurdjieff Foundation. The office was at the end of the hall, on the fourth floor. There was a glossy black door with gold lettering: American British Electric Corporation and, below that, Hunting Surveys and Consultants.

The suite was laid out in a spacious square; three of the quadrants formed an open area, and the fourth was Lord Pentland's private office. The reception area—separated from Lord Pentland's office by an interior wall—had a faded oriental carpet, a row of old-fashioned metal filing cabinets, and two green chairs flanking a small table where people would sit, stiff and nervous, while they waited to see him. On the wall were old black-and-white aerial photographs taken by Hunting Surveys. On my first day as secretary, Lord Pentland asked me to take two of them to a nearby print-and-framing shop to see if the owner was interested in purchasing them. I knew nothing about the photographs or why anyone would want them, and had no idea what price to ask. I wasn't able to sell them, though I did try, and Lord Pentland seemed satisfied with my attempt. Later we took them down and replaced them with newer, more colorful photos.

There were five wooden desks with black rectangular surfaces, reputedly from a Frank Lloyd Wright design: one in Lord Pentland's office, one for Dick Brower, one in the reception area that we used for lunch, and two joined at right angles for me and my bright blue IBM selectric typewriter, a high-tech piece of equipment that stood out among the rather old-fashioned decor. The desktops were made of a distinctive material that seemed designed to record every lapse of attention. Each time I set down a hot coffee cup or pressed too hard with a pencil, a permanent mark appeared on the surface. My desk looked battered and pock-marked—in contrast with Lord Pentland's, which remained pristine.

On Lord Pentland's desk—in addition to a few practical items, including a telephone, a small wind-up clock, and a lamp with an ivory shade—there was a collection of carved elephants and a photo of his daughter Mary. Behind him, on a shelf under the window, a round pewter tin held the Godiva chocolates that he offered to his visitors. One of my tasks was to make sure that the tin was always filled.

I remember the sense of order I felt each morning as I went into Lord Pentland's office to turn on his desk lamp and wind the clock. It was an orderliness that helped to ground me. Rather than feeling automatic, the routine brought me back to myself and why I was there.

Although Lord Pentland didn't generally appear until about ten, he would often phone at precisely nine o'clock and greet me with exaggerated surprise. "Oh, you're there!" I don't recall ever being late, yet there was always a moment of panic when I unlocked the office door and slid open the coat closet: if Lord Pentland's hat was on the shelf, it meant he had arrived first; no hat, and there was time to prepare. Promptness was important, and he rarely kept anyone waiting.

Sometimes Lord Pentland would return to his apartment for lunch and a rest; sometimes we had lunch in the office. He might ask me to go out and get some bread, cheese, avocado, and tomato for a sandwich, or little tub of chicken salad with grapes. Lunch was a time to relax. Lord Pentland would talk about items in the news—he read the *New York Times* every morning, as soon as he arrived—or plans for weekend activities, but rarely about Work ideas. Sometimes, though, he would "try out" an idea on Dick and me that he would bring up later in my group meeting and then, on a broader scale, on a Tuesday night panel.

As we sat there eating, I would try desperately to think of topics in that elusive middle realm, neither too serious nor too personal, to engage him in conversation. I was young, however, with no experience in the art of conversation, and there were times when I couldn't think of a thing to say. Lord Pentland would eat his lunch in silence, his face expressionless.

On occasion, he would have lunch in his private office with someone who had come to meet with him. I especially remember the lunches he would have with Bill Segal, one of his peers at the Foundation, whose company Lord Pentland seemed to genuinely enjoy. The two men would spend a long time together, door closed, and emerge relaxed and laughing, thanking me with utmost graciousness for the lunch, though all I'd done was to buy the food and put it on plates.

Back then, in the late 1970s and early 1980s we had no computers, printers, or email. When I typed a letter—on one of several letterheads, depending on its purpose—I had to make carbon copies for the files: pink for Hunting business, blue for American British, green for Foundation-related correspondence. I would arrange the typed letters on Lord Pentland's desk, from left to right: one vertical row for Triangle Editions (relating to the Gurdjieff books), another for Remar Productions (relating to the *Meetings with Remarkable Men* film), and a third for his personal letters.

Incoming mail was arranged in the same way, each letter paper-clipped to its envelope. Lord Pentland asked me to open his letters, no matter who they were from. He never said, "Don't read them." That seemed obvious, and I never did.

Lord Pentland corresponded with a wide range of people in Europe and the U.S., nearly always replying the same day. He also wrote extensively on subjects ranging from money, food, and fatigue to the history of Gurdjieff's ideas. Since Lord Pentland did a great deal of writing—letters, notes for talks he was giving, essays destined for print—I did a great deal of typing. The IBM selectric was faster than the manual typewriter I was used to, but there was no easy way to correct a mistake or edit a sentence. Mistakes had to be fixed with a tiny brushful of Wite-Out, exactly the right amount to cover the mistake without leaking onto adjacent letters. I had to wait until the paint dried and then reinsert the paper, aligning it by hand so the strike of the key would fall exactly into place. Revisions meant typing the whole letter or essay from the beginning.

There were always many things going on at once—letters from people in France and England and California about the Gurdjieff Work, perhaps an inquiry from someone about the history of the Sinclair clan, phone calls from people wanting to meet with Lord Pentland, as well as telexes and calls about projects for Hunting.

The juxtaposition of Work and life—the coexistence of Lord Pentland's activities on behalf of the Gurdjieff teaching and the needs of the firm that was paying the rent—required a supple alertness, an attention to a business memo that was just as rigorous as the attention I gave to a paragraph composed by Lord Pentland himself. He didn't so, not in words, but I always felt that each depended on the other. To be sloppy in a business matter would jeopardize our presence as guests in an office that we were permitted to occupy, thanks to Hunting's generosity, and deprive Lord Pentland of a place to oversee the Gurdjieff books, music, films, and international relations. In the same way, the care I took with business tasks would support the Work—how I held the silver letter-opener to slit open an envelope or pressed a stamp to the special sponge we used for the quarterly mailing of the Hunting magazine.

There was a door from the main area to Lord Pentland's private office but he rarely shut it, only when he was meeting privately with someone in one of his groups. Otherwise, whether he was writing or on the phone, he left it open. When he needed me, he would lift his head and ask me to come in. He never raised his voice, yet I always heard it.

I can still see him—an old man at his desk, writing and thinking, a yellow pool of light from the desk lamp shining on the top of his head and the pad of paper in front of him. Like Gurdjieff in the café, I think Lord Pentland liked working in the midst of the business world. Certainly, the geophysical business was always more active when he was in town. Dick and I both remarked on that—as if the energy of inner work that Lord Pentland generated also attracted the energy of outer life.

Although Lord Pentland could easily have written letters, made phone calls, met with people, and taken care of his various endeavors at the Gurdjieff Foundation or his apartment on Sixty-Sixth Street, he came to the Madison Avenue office nearly every day. I don't believe he would have done that if he hadn't found it helpful.

As I reflect on those years, it strikes me that it was a period characterized, in general, by a new outreach into the wider world. Weekend activities for Lord Pentland's groups moved from the seclusion of an elegant estate in Armonk to a converted firehouse in Sparkill, a small town on the Hudson. Unlike the Armonk property, the building was located right in the center of town—next to a store that sold wood-burning stoves and across from the post office—and provided a kind of middle ground between the special atmosphere of the Foundation and "regular life."

So too, my first year in the office was marked by the launch of the *Meetings with Remarkable Men* film, the first film about the Gurdjieff teaching intended for public viewing. Groups in each city where it was being shown were asked to help with promotion by distributing flyers and posters; in New York, someone was scheduled to attend each performance and report on the audience reaction. The office at 790 Madison Avenue was also the headquarters for Remar Productions, the company formed to oversee the film's distribution.

During this period, Lord Pentland gave a number of talks to groups outside the Foundation. Work was also underway to make the records and cassettes of the Gurdjieff-de Hartmann music available to the general public, although that project wasn't completed until a year after his death.

The Beginning
November 1978

Before I came to New York to be Lord Pentland's secretary, I was living in Berkeley, California, and attending the Gurdjieff group at the San Francisco mansion known as "St. Elmo," after the street it was on.

Although I'd met with Lord Pentland a few times over the years, I was far from his intimate circle and he had never paid me any particular attention—not until the day in the St. Elmo library when I asked Jerry Needleman, as Jacob Needleman was called, whether he wanted a document single-spaced or double-spaced. Needleman, one of the senior people in the San Francisco Foundation, was overseeing a project about the history of the Work in America. I had been helping with small tasks like typing index cards and taking photos from private collections to be professionally copied.

My question echoed in the silence of the library, and I felt Lord Pentland raise his eyes from the table where he sat writing. It was a palpable sensation, as if his antennae went up and fixed on me, someone he hadn't really noticed before.

The next day, the phone rang in my Berkeley apartment. I recognized the voice at once, though it hardly seemed possible that he was calling. "Is that Barbara? This is Lord Pentland."

He paused for an instant before identifying himself as *Lord Pentland*. I had the distinct impression that he had done it for my sake, knowing that *John Pentland,* the name he used, would have sounded strange to me.

My response was—in a word—pure terror. What awful thing had I done to cause the president of the Foundation to call me personally? I was certain that I was going to be expelled from the Work. But Lord Pentland merely asked if I could come to see him at his apartment at St. Elmo, where he stayed when he was in town. I knew where the apartment was but had never been inside. Still terrified, I agreed.

When I arrived at the appointed time, Lord Pentland greeted me, offered me a seat, and excused himself for a moment. He went into a bathroom adjacent to the sitting room. Then, to my horror, I heard him urinate.

That unmistakable sound, after my initial shock, brought about a sudden and equally unmistakable shift in my inner state, as panic gave way to the undeniable fact of Lord Pentland's humanity.

Perhaps it sounds odd that I'd never thought of Lord Pentland as a human being, but I hadn't. He was a master, an avatar, a figure so far above my own level of being that the notion of him as *also a man* hadn't occurred to me. Although I didn't appreciate the significance of this shift in awareness—not at the moment it happened—it became apparent early in my tenure as his secretary that this impression of Lord Pentland *as a man* was absolutely crucial. Without it, I would have been unable to fulfill my role and be useful to him.

When Lord Pentland returned to the sitting room, he reached for a box of chocolates. "Have one," he said. "It'll help you relax while you prepare."

Relax? I let out my breath and told him, "I'd have to eat the whole box."

He nodded. "I understand." Then he asked if I could drive him to a geophysics convention in downtown San Francisco. The request seemed strange, since it had nothing to do with the Gurdjieff Work, but I said yes, of course. We walked to my car, which was parked nearby.

As I discovered, we were headed to the annual gathering of the Society for Exploration Geophysicists (SEG), of which Lord Pentland was a member. He and Dick Brower had a booth representing American British Electric, which was still an active company.

When we arrived at the convention center, a guard asked for our passes. Lord Pentland produced his, and then turned to me. "Why don't you get yourself a guest pass or something and meet me inside?"

He handed me a nametag that said: *John Pentland, American British Electric Corporation*. He gestured in the direction of a reception desk at the far end of the lobby and then strode off, toward an escalator that led to the exhibition hall downstairs.

I raced to the reception desk, showed the attendant his nametag, and said, "I need a guest pass, please"—all the while trying to keep track of Lord Pentland's rapidly disappearing figure. Distracted by a phone call, the attendant typed something quickly and pushed it across the counter. It was an entry pass with the words: *Joan Pentland*. A small tilt in a single letter, two lines meeting at the apex instead of standing parallel, a receptionist's assumption—and I was in.

Waving the pass at the guard, I ran after Lord Pentland and somehow, miraculously, caught up with him just as he was about to vanish into the crowd. He turned to me with a huge smile that grew even more delighted when I showed him what the receptionist had typed.

Then he motioned for me to come with him, and we strolled through several aisles until we came to a booth manned by Dick Brower. Lord Pentland introduced us and explained about the company and the SEG. As surreal as it felt to be at a geophysics convention with Lord Pentland, my sense of theater—of something artificial and staged—grew even stronger when he draped his arm around my shoulder with exaggerated casualness and drawled, "So, Dick, I had this crazy idea that I might ask Barbara to come to New York and be my secretary."

Dick looked startled, then collected himself and said something noncommittal. Lord Pentland turned and asked what I thought.

I had no idea how to reply. In my wildest imagination, I had never envisioned anything like this. I tried to remember what people were supposed to say when they were offered a job. Somehow, the first words out of my mouth were: "How much would you pay me?"

To say that the audacity of the question appalled me is an understatement, although I suspect that it amused Lord Pentland. He told me what he paid his current secretary and said he would pay me the same amount. The number barely registered. I was too stunned by what was happening.

Then he asked if I thought I could get along with Dick—to which I replied *yes*, not knowing Dick and not knowing what else to say—and added that I could come for six weeks while his secretary was on maternity leave and see how it went. He told me to think about it and come to see him the following day with my answer. Then he thanked me for the ride and said he would get a lift back to St. Elmo with Dick.

There was no question in my mind that I would accept Lord Pentland's offer, but I was glad for a day to digest what had taken place. When I returned to his apartment the next afternoon, I told him that it felt like falling in love, with the same quality of enchantment. He said it was true, but I had to be careful.

Lord Pentland's previous secretaries had come from San Francisco, so he may have been on the lookout, during his visit, for a likely replacement. With no child or husband or job to bind me to the Bay Area, I was a reasonable choice, despite my lack of experience.

Although I admit to thinking so at first, I quickly understood that the "guest pass" wasn't a test I had to pass before Lord Pentland offered me the job. Rather, it may have been a way for him to observe me in the midst of life. Perhaps he wanted to see what I would do and what I would attract. Was I someone who attracted "good luck" or someone who attracted complications and obstacles? Either, I think, could have been interesting to him.

All I can really say—looking back on this extraordinary turn of events—is that I was in the right place at the right time and, as it turned out, had qualities that could be useful in a secretary. I remember Lord Pentland asking me, during our ride to the SEG convention, what I was good at. I had recently left a teaching job to try writing short stories, so I said, "Well, I hope I'm a good writer."

Lord Pentland threw me a look of irritation. It was obvious that wasn't what he was interested in, so I added, "I'm good at organizing things." This time he nodded, apparently satisfied. In any case, he didn't press me further.

He gave me two secretarial tasks the following day, when I returned to accept the job. The first was a handwritten essay that he wanted me to type.

I stared at the endless string of seemingly-identical vertical strokes, not comprehending how they could possibly represent anything in the English language. Then, suddenly, as if a lens had shifted, my eyes relaxed, the shapes separated into letters and words, and I understood how to "read" his handwriting—*because I had to.*

Then he gave me an envelope addressed to Madame de Salzmann in Paris and asked me to drop it in the mail. I took the letter, awed by the responsibility, since Madame de Salzmann was Gurdjieff's appointed successor and the most revered embodiment of his teaching, not only in France but throughout the world.

After I left St. Elmo, however, I noticed that Lord Pentland had put a domestic stamp on the envelope. Was *this* the test, to see if I'd notice and fix the mistake—or should I be a humble student and mail it anyway? The latter seemed like a stupid thing to do, so I went to the post office, bought an international stamp, and dropped the letter in the box.

Part of me wanted to let Lord Pentland know what had happened so he would see how attentive I was; at the same time, that felt sleazy and self-serving. The image of my own cleverness in catching the error was like a burning coal, rationalized by the conviction that I ought to assure him that his letter to Madame de Salzmann would arrive safely. I ended up telling him about the stamp the next day. He seemed uninterested.

Lord Pentland arranged for me to stay with Dianne Edenfield, secretary of the New York Foundation, during my six-week "trial period." Dianne had a large apartment on the Upper East Side with a room suitable for a guest.

I had never lived in a big city, and Manhattan was magical. The quiet beauty of the snow-covered streets as I walked to work. The hiss of the radiators in Dianne's apartment, releasing so much steam that we had to keep the windows cracked, despite the freezing temperature. The black-clad elegance of the people at the New York Foundation, after the India prints and gypsy shawls of California.

Wendy Bayne, Lord Pentland's previous secretary, had her baby a week after my arrival, but I didn't know if he intended her to return. He had told me to come for six weeks. Did that mean I would be shooed away after six weeks had passed, back to San Francisco, so Wendy could resume her post? Hoping for anything else felt greedy, presumptuous. In any case, it was up to Lord Pentland, not me. And yet a question hovered in the air, just beyond my reach.

I didn't hear it—not even when Lord Pentland remarked, as if making a casual observation: "I won't take Wendy back, you know. Her husband needs to find a way to support her." I nodded stupidly, too slow and passive to see the obvious.

The six weeks were almost over before I understood: Lord Pentland wasn't going to invite me to stay. I had to ask. And if I was too timid to take that step, I would go back to Berkeley and that would be that.

I had to be an adult instead of a little girl—shift from being a deferential visitor to someone active enough to be useful to him.

When I asked, finally, if I could continue as his secretary, he looked as if I'd proposed something astonishing. Then he asked how long I would need to settle everything in California. Two weeks, I told him. I'd be back right after the new year.

I returned to San Francisco to sell my furniture and most of my belongings, find a home for my dog, pack, move. My flight to JFK was on New Year's Eve as 1978 slid into 1979.

I found a studio apartment at 79th and York. I had no furniture, not at first—it was too expensive to ship furniture from the West Coast. While I waited for my new sofa bed to arrive, Lord Pentland offered to loan me the horsehair mattress he had used at Cambridge. I retrieved the mattress from the storage cage in the basement of his building and brought it to my apartment in a taxi.

Once the furniture was installed, I had a housewarming party. I invited Lord Pentland and, to my amazement, he came.

I can still see him sitting on the end of the gray and peach-colored couch, with the *full-to-the-rim* coffee cup I'd poured for him balanced on his right knee. He sat there for over an hour, the cup immobile, as people came to sit beside him—each hoping for a bit of conversation, each sinking into the cushion in a different way and displacing it again when they rose. I didn't dare to replace the cup with one he might actually be able to drink from, too fearful that I would spill coffee on his leg.

Finally, mercifully, he handed me the cup just before he left—not a drop splashed on the saucer or even a ripple on the surface of the liquid—and thanked me for inviting him.

It was a small impression, yet the way Lord Pentland dealt with the coffee cup—and his overzealous hostess—was the way he seemed to deal with whatever came his way: as an opportunity for his own work. Sometimes I was alert enough to notice, sometimes I wasn't.

Writing this, decades later, I'm struck with how Lord Pentland acted, from the very beginning, as if he trusted me. He made no attempt to hide anything or keep any secrets; his correspondence was in full view, along with his private files. He rarely closed the door when he was on the phone and often asked me to deliver personal messages.

There was no way for Lord Pentland to "know" if I was trustworthy. Perhaps he decided to act as if I were and see what happened. That would fit what I observed, time and again—how he rarely interfered with something that was already in motion, even if it was clear that it was going to go badly.

In short: he had hired me. Having done that, we would see how it went.

Despite a lack of secretarial training, I did find ways to carry out the tasks I was given. For example, I developed my own system for taking dictation consisting mainly of squiggles and abbreviations, an elaboration of the *ad hoc* shorthand I'd concocted during years of taking notes in group meetings.

In case I got too comfortable with my makeshift secretarial skills, however, Lord Pentland liked to point to Stephen Grant, the attorney who oversaw Foundation matters and was one of the people whose counsel Lord Pentland relied on.

As Lord Pentland enjoyed reminding me: "Stephen used to have a secretary in the Work, but he's come up in the world."

Impressions

A Paper Clip on the Carpet

I returned to New York, no longer there on a temporary basis but officially Lord Pentland's secretary. Soon afterward, David Sinker came to visit. Sinker was the chief executive officer at Hunting Surveys and Consultants, the British company that was, by then, the sole firm that American British Electric was representing. He had come for a critical meeting with Lord Pentland that would determine whether Hunting would assume responsibility for the office.

As someone inexperienced in the business world, I had no idea of the long and careful preparation Lord Pentland had put into this transition. If successful, it would allow him to retire with an office where he could conduct other business on behalf of the Gurdjieff Work while assuring that his company would continue under the aegis of a larger firm. If the meeting had gone badly, the office would have had to shut down because there was no way, at that point, for American British to generate enough income to cover expenses, including a Madison Avenue rent. Much was at stake for all three of us—Lord Pentland, Dick, and myself—but I was unaware of that too. All I knew was that there was a heightened alertness as we waited for David Sinker to appear.

Earlier that morning, Lord Pentland had made a seemingly casual remark about how attentive Sinker was. I remember wondering, fleetingly, why he had said that, before dismissing the comment and returning to my task. A bit later, as I was bringing some papers to him, I half-noticed a paper clip on the carpet. I didn't stop, though—too caught in the momentum of crossing the room with the pile of letters I had typed so carefully.

When David Sinker arrived, he shook hands with Dick and me, then followed Lord Pentland across the reception area to his private office. To my horror, he bent down and picked up a paper clip—the very paper clip I'd ignored—and handed it to me. It was a small thing, hardly important enough to ruin the negotiations, yet it gave a subtle impression of carelessness and imprecision. Had Lord Pentland noticed the paper clip and offered a reminder that could have awakened me from my passivity? Had he foreseen? Or was he making a general statement, and the paper clip was simply a coincidence?

There was no way to know, but the moment has remained with me—David Sinker silently dropping a paper clip into my outstretched hand.

The negotiations were successful. My little paper clip didn't "matter" enough to ruin the years of service that Lord Pentland had provided. But it mattered to me, a tangible indicator of my state of "waking sleep."

Words

Soon after Sinker's visit, Lord Pentland told me a story about a woman who had caused her company to lose a million-dollar contract by mixing up letters to Shell and Exxon, rival oil companies, and putting them in the wrong envelopes. I had no idea if the story was true, but I thought of it each time I was about to seal an envelope, whether it was to someone at the World Bank or someone in the Paris group. The question seemed to echo in the big square room: "Are you sure you haven't mixed them up?"

Occasionally Lord Pentland would change his mind about something he had written and have me re-type a sealed letter before it was mailed, suggesting that I steam off the stamp and re-use it on a fresh envelope. The suggestion might sound humorous, evidence of a Scottish frugality, but his remark made me wonder: What would it be, not to waste anything?

Lord Pentland maintained an active and eclectic correspondence, writing many of his letters, as well as drafts of his essays, in longhand on a ruled yellow pad. At other times, he dictated while I faced him across the polished black desk. Although he spoke at a steady, unhurried pace, he rarely stopped until he had come to the end of whatever he was composing. Thus, there was seldom a gap when I could "go back and fill in" what I had missed. What helped, given my lack of secretarial skills, was to stay with his voice, at the tempo of his speech, neither anticipating nor trying to catch up. If I could remain attentive like that, the pen seemed to move by itself and record the word at the very instant it was spoken.

Lord Pentland would often ask me to read back what he had dictated, and then stop me to change a word or a phrase. He did the same thing when revising what I had typed. It was striking to see how the substitution or addition of a single word could change the whole meaning of the sentence—to witness the elegance and precision of his intelligence.

There were several times when I "corrected" something while typing a paragraph he had dictated, thinking that he had accidentally added or omitted a word. He always caught my hubris when he read the typed page and restored the original language.

Like each paper clip and stamp, each word mattered.

It's Just the Cat

As Wendy, my predecessor, had explained, Lord Pentland took coffee at eleven o'clock every morning, whether he was on the phone, in a meeting, or working quietly at his desk. It ought to have been a simple task, but in the beginning I was timid rather than direct, and turned the coffee service into an absurd imposition.

Fearful of interrupting, I'd hover nervously outside his private office, waiting for just the right moment to ask if he wanted coffee—even though it was eleven o'clock and I knew very well that he wanted coffee. No doubt he felt me hovering, but he wouldn't look up and acknowledge me. Eventually I would have to interrupt him—the very thing I dreaded doing, and the very opposite of the thoughtful simplicity that was called for—and he would have to say, "Yes, please."

Then I went to the other extreme and prepared what I thought he "deserved"—a beautiful tray with a creamer of half-and-half, a little blue teapot, a silver spoon, and a napkin-covered plate of cookies. The tray took up far too much room on his desk and required him to rearrange his papers. Still, I was unwilling to give up my idea of how beautifully I wanted to serve him.

This continued until the day, trying to balance too much, that I dropped everything all over his desk while Lord Pentland was speaking on the phone. Cups and dishes crashed and banged as hot liquid spilled across his desk. Lord Pentland withdrew a few inches to avoid the mess and told the person he was speaking with: "Don't mind the noise. It's just the cat."

The Telephone

Since Hunting was now paying my salary, Lord Pentland was meticulous in giving priority to Hunting's needs. If he was in the midst of dictating a letter and the phone rang, he would nod for me to answer. When it was a business matter, I had to attend to it and keep him waiting, excruciating as that was. Then, as soon as the call was over, he would pick up where he had left off, even if it was in the middle of a sentence.

I never knew who might be calling or what the call might be about—a question from someone in one of Lord Pentland's groups; an inquiry about the Gurdjieff books or music; a business request from Dave Francis or Derek Morris, heads of the Hunting branches in England, or one of their contacts in Washington. I always answered "9600" (the last four digits of the phone number), a generic response that revealed nothing.

If the call was for Lord Pentland, the "rule" was that I had to ask before putting anyone through or revealing if he was in. The only exceptions were Madame de Salzmann and his daughter Mary. Otherwise, I had to say, "Let me see if Lord Pentland is there" and press the *hold* button while I told him who it was. Sometimes he would accept the call; sometimes he wouldn't. He might say, "Oh, what's that S.O.B. want?" and then take the phone from my hand, oozing graciousness as he greeted the caller.

If I slipped and said, "I'll see if he's free"—implying that he was there—he would tell me to say that he wasn't in. I'd have to get back on the line and sound like an idiot or a liar. "Actually, he's not here right now"— as if I hadn't known whether or not he was in the very same office, only steps away.

One time, someone in Group One—the most senior people in

the Foundation, those who had worked directly with Gurdjieff—insisted that she had to talk to him. She kept asking when he would be in, where he was, when he was expected. Even though he was sitting right across from me, I had to keep replying that I didn't know. Finally, she snapped, "What kind of secretary are you, anyway?"

I felt certain that Lord Pentland could tell from my defensive posture that she was trying to get me to crack, but he didn't say a word. He merely waited for me to finish, and then resumed what we had been doing.

I wasn't always that resolute. On more than one occasion, Lord Pentland showed me how easily I lost myself, just because someone "important" was on the line.

There was the time, for instance, when I was sitting across from Lord Pentland as he dictated an essay and the phone rang. It was Henri Tracol, a senior member of the French Foundation, calling from Paris. In the politest manner imaginable, he asked if he might possibly speak with Lord Pentland. "Oh yes, Mr. Tracol!" I exclaimed. "He's right here."

As I handed the phone to Lord Pentland, he looked at me with utter contempt. "My God, you're weak," he said.

Obedience

While Lord Pentland expected me to reply as instructed when someone called and to record his words exactly as he uttered them, he also expected me to have common sense—to serve, but not stupidly. The balance between these two directives, obedience and judgment, required a discernment that I had to learn. The lessons came in unexpected and memorable ways.

One illustrative incident took place in early January of 1979. As happened each year, plans were underway for the January 13 celebration of Mr. Gurdjieff's birthday. The centerpiece of that year's event was the inaugural screening of the *Meetings with Remarkable Men* film—after years of preparation and anticipation—for members of the New York Foundation.

The woman in charge of arrangements with the auditorium at the Metropolitan Museum of Art, which had been rented for the occasion, had called numerous times with questions for Lord Pentland, since no one dared to make the smallest decision without consulting him. She was a particular type, anxious and aggressive at the same time, and every question was urgent.

When she called, yet again, I pressed the *hold* button and told Lord Pentland, "So-and-so is on the phone."

He gave me a deadpan look. "Oh, tell her to go fuck herself."

Absurd as it sounds now, I actually wondered if I was supposed to repeat his exact words—if that was what an obedient secretary, and pupil, was meant to do. The seconds seemed endless as he waited for me to release the *hold* button and relay his message.

Finally, I returned to the line and said, "Lord Pentland can't come to the phone right now. May I take a message?"

He never said anything like that in my presence again.

The Key

Lord Pentland told me a story about Thelma Titus, secretary at the Gurdjieff Foundation in San Francisco. He had, apparently, given Thelma the only key to a special file cabinet, with the instruction not to give the key to anyone, no matter who it was or why they said they needed it. One day, he asked her to give him the key because he had to get something out of the cabinet, but she refused. Not even him, even though it was *his* key and *his* files!

As he related the story and seemed to marvel at Thelma's steadfastness, the point wasn't at all clear to me. Did he mean that Thelma had been strong and honorable, or rigid and silly? Was I supposed to emulate her or exercise more intelligence?

Perhaps I should have asked, but I didn't. Like the story of the woman who'd put the letter to Exxon in an envelope addressed to Shell, Lord Pentland's anecdotes—always related in the driest, most casual manner—were as deft as those of a Zen master.

I faced a similar dilemma each time he asked for a cigarette. In those days, I smoked a distinctive brand of cigarette made by Nat Sherman that was long, thin, and wrapped in a special dark brown paper. Lord Pentland wasn't supposed to smoke, but on occasion he would stroll over to my desk, hands in his pockets, and say, "Oh Barbara, can you spare one of your beautiful little cigars? I really need one right now."

The first time he did that, I had no idea how to respond. Was I supposed to refuse, remind him that it wasn't allowed, and put his health first, no matter how innocent and beguiling he seemed? To be as steadfast in the face of his own request as I'd learned to be with the members of Group One—like Thelma and the key, but with more at stake because it was a matter of his wellbeing? What would a friend do, someone who cared about him?

I looked at him—and understood that he was telling the truth. It had been a long, demanding day. He was tired and needed a cigarette.

The moment in his apartment at St. Elmo came back to me, when I realized that he was human, a man. I gave him the cigarette.

Gifts

Dianne Edenfield, the Foundation secretary with whom I stayed during those early weeks, mentioned that Lord Pentland enjoyed the treats she sometimes baked for him. Spurred by her example—and, of course, wanting to do equally well—I made a pan of date nut bars and presented them to him the following day.

Lord Pentland took the pan and put it on the windowsill, not even removing the foil to see what was inside. I watched him, confused and disappointed, as I waited for the expression of pleasure that never came.

Shame replaced confusion later that morning when Lord Pentland gave the pan of date bars to his very first visitor, a woman from London with no connection to the Gurdjieff Work. As I watched her stride out of the office, happily bearing the "lovely gift" he had given her, I was faced, belatedly, with my own insincerity.

Lord Pentland hadn't said a word, but I understood: there was no feeling in the date bars, only imitation and ambition. That made them, for him, inedible.

In contrast, he was unfailingly appreciative when I ran to the corner market to buy some bread, cheese, and avocado for his lunch. An enormous smile would spread across his face as he reached for the plate where I'd arranged the items. "How do you ever manage to make something so delicious?" he would exclaim.

I always felt awkward when he said that—an imposter, praised for "nothing"—even though there was no irony in his voice.

Yet there was an occasion when I did give him something that he accepted, and he gave me a gift in return. Shortly after the incident with the date bars, Lord Pentland asked me to take a painting that someone had made for him and find out how much it would cost to have it framed. I went to a few framing shops, but he said their prices were too steep.

I decided to take the painting to a place I'd noticed on my way to work called *Make-a-Frame*. Although it doesn't exist anymore, *Make-a-Frame* was a framing shop with a do-it-yourself section where customers could proceed through a series of "stations" and frame their own pictures. The process was more complicated than I'd realized, but I emerged at the end of Saturday afternoon with a framed painting. When I gave it to Lord Pentland the following Monday and told him how I'd made it (and at a cheap price), he seemed very pleased.

He went home for lunch and came back with a framed poster of a Tibetan thangka that his friend, Tibetan scholar Lobsang Lhalungpa, had given him. "You can have this one if you like," he said. "I don't need it anymore."

At the Elevator

Although Lord Pentland always had coffee at eleven o'clock, the rest of his schedule varied. He would often leave the office at three o'clock to rest before an evening of activities at the Foundation, but on occasion he would remain until five o'clock to finish something he was working on.

Late one afternoon, the phone rang a few moments after Lord Pentland had left for the day. It was one of his peers, a woman from the most senior group at the Foundation.

"I'm so sorry," I told her. "He's just left."

"Oh no," she said. "Are you sure you can't catch him?"

Her disappointment, coupled with the challenge she had offered, was a hook I couldn't resist. "Let me see." I placed the phone on the desk and raced down the hall, spotting Lord Pentland as he was about to step into the elevator.

"Lord Pentland, Lord Pentland!" I shouted, out of breath but feeling quite heroic. "So-and-so is on the phone for you!"

Instead of praising me for catching him before he missed an important call, he looked at me in disgust. "You've ruined my whole day," he told me.

Mortified, I followed him down the hall, back to the office. He picked up the phone, greeting the woman with utmost sweetness and charm, then left—for the second time—without glancing at me.

I sank into my desk chair, flooded with despair at the reality of my own sleep. I had completely forgotten my role—my very presence—in a moment of what Gurdjieff calls identification with the idea of being "helpful" to someone who had, in fact, called after five o'clock.

My sense of duty and purpose was no match for the woman's cleverness in knowing exactly how to flatter me into siding with her. I knew very well that Lord Pentland disliked backtracking: if you've left the office, you've left the office. That was why, I think, he held the view on abortion that he shared with me later. He told me that he wasn't against abortion *per se*, although he was against stopping what had been started.

In general, my impression was that Lord Pentland favored letting things play out, without interference. When people asked for his advice on personal matters, he would rarely tell them what to do. There was one instance, for example, when a woman who was involved in a rather destructive relationship came to ask Lord Pentland what she should do, but he refused to offer any opinion.

Nor would he react when people announced that they'd had enough of a difficult situation. Whenever Henry Jacobson, who was helping to promote the *Meetings with Remarkable Men* film, submitted a long and heartfelt letter of resignation—which he did every so often—Lord Pentland would tell me: "Put it in the file."

Henry would call later that day to ask about Lord Pentland's response to his letter, and I would have to say: "He told me to file it." That was all Lord Pentland ever said, and Henry always appeared the next day to continue his task.

Another time, I was upset about a personal situation and wanted desperately to do something about it. But Lord Pentland told me: "You have to let the apple fall from the tree."

Get Him on the Phone

It was clear to me, as it was to others who spent time with him, that Lord Pentland was someone who lived with intention.

By *intention* I don't mean the hopeful, future-oriented *making-of-plans,* as in a "good intention" that ends up having a contrary result. Rather, the intention that accompanied Lord Pentland was of an entirely different order, perceptible as a quality of vibration that emanated from his presence. It seemed to come from another source, moving through him—like a magnetic field that penetrated, vivified, and transformed the state of those around him as well.

Opening to that vibration and obeying its call seemed to produce a special kind of "coincidence" that made things work out in ways that appeared miraculous. This point is crucial. Otherwise, the stories below might sound as if they are about my own heroism. They are not; they are examples of how Lord Pentland created a necessity, through the quality of his intention, that enabled those around him to align with his will and carry out what was required.

There was the time, for example, when Peter Brook was in town preparing for a production of *Carmen* at Lincoln Center. Peter was—and is—one of the world's mostly highly-acclaimed theatre directors. He was also deeply involved in the Gurdjieff Work and directed the *Meetings with Remarkable Men* film under Madame de Salzmann's guidance.

Lord Pentland called me into his office and said, "Get Peter on the phone." I didn't know where Peter was, but guessed that he was rehearsing. I dialed the number for Lincoln Center. After endless rings, someone answered. I begged and bullied and insisted, and finally the operator put me through to a phone backstage.

However, the stagehand told me: "There's no way Mr. Brook can be interrupted. They're in the final dress rehearsal. I can give him a message when they take a break, but I don't know when that will be."

That wasn't good enough. I was going to get Peter on the phone and that was that. I steeled myself and insisted: "Tell Mr. Brook that Lord Pentland is calling, and I guarantee on my life that he'll take the call."

The stagehand did get Peter, and Peter did take the call—not because I was clever or determined, but because *Lord Pentland needed to talk to him*.

On another occasion, Lord Pentland was on the phone in his private office when he motioned for me to come in. He handed me his Day-at-a-Glance appointment book from the previous year. "You remember that film maker who came to see me last fall? Find his phone number for me." He held the phone away from his ear. "I'll wait."

Slowly, I walked back to my desk with the appointment book. I did remember a film maker coming to see Lord Pentland the previous year, but I had no idea of the man's name or even the month of his visit—and there was Lord Pentland, the telephone receiver a few inches from his ear, waiting for me to return with the number.

I stood absolutely still, feeling the force of his unflinching gaze. Then something shifted inside and I opened the diary, right to the page with the man's name and number. I copied the information onto a piece of paper and gave it to Lord Pentland, who barely glanced my way and resumed his conversation.

Peter Brook's Pants

Another time, Peter was meeting with Lord Pentland in his private office. They had been sequestered for a while when Lord Pentland opened the door and announced loudly: "Oh, don't worry, Barbara can take care of it. She can fix anything." By then I knew enough to be warned, not flattered, by a pronouncement like that.

The hem had come out on the left leg of Peter's pants. Lord Pentland asked if I had a needle and thread, and I said that I did. He pulled a chair up to my desk, and Peter propped his foot on the seat while the two of them continued their discussion, standing casually in the middle of the room as if there was nothing unusual about the context of their conversation.

I threaded a needle, crouched on the carpet, and began to make my way around the circumference of the hem. It was an irresistible opportunity to eavesdrop on an exchange between two men whose words were, to say the least, utterly compelling. I tried to be inconspicuous as I—literally—crawled at their feet.

It was a unique experience. On the one hand, I couldn't help being drawn by all the interesting things they were saying. At the same time, I couldn't be *so* interested that I lost my concentration and stabbed Peter with the needle.

Although I no longer recall what they said, I'll never forget how it felt to crawl along the rug, twisting my neck as I held the fabric away from Peter's ankle and pushed the needle through to the other side. I was keenly aware that there would be no ripping-out, backtracking, or doing it better a second time. All I had was one stitch at a time.

The Hat

Lord Pentland's hat was like a part of him. It was an old-fashioned, rather shabby brown hat that he wore every day during the chilly months from October to April. I can still see the hat on the closet shelf, on the far left, or in profile as he strode down the street. It was personal, intimate, a symbol of Lord Pentland himself—so deeply tied to him that when he died, his daughter Mary placed the hat on top of the coffin and buried it with him.

The notion of Lord Pentland losing his hat seems unthinkable, yet it nearly happened.

The saga began on a Friday evening when I went to a performance-in-the-round at the New York Open Center. To my surprise, Lord Pentland and a companion were seated on the other side of the stage, directly across from me. I caught his eye, then looked way, sensing that he wanted me to respect his privacy. I didn't speak to him or make any further contact for the rest of the evening.

On Monday morning, Lord Pentland came into the office and said, "You saw where I was sitting the other night? Well, I think I left my hat there. I put it under the seat during the show. Do you think you could go 'round and fetch it for me?"

My heart sank. It had been more than two days—an entire weekend, with multiple performances on Saturday and Sunday. I was sure that someone had cleaned the theatre since Friday night. The image of a janitor finding Lord Pentland's hat and throwing it away—or, worse, taking it home and wearing it—was too awful to contemplate. But I said yes, of course.

When I got to the theatre, it was closed. It was a Monday, when theatres are dark. Eventually I found someone in the office and convinced him to let me in. He waited in the doorway as I stood surveying the empty auditorium with its rows of identical seats circling the now-barren stage. There was nothing to orient me in the vacant sameness of a theatre-in-the-round, and I had a moment of near-panic when I couldn't remember where Lord Pentland had been sitting. Finally, on instinct, I walked to a row that felt right.

The floor was spotless; clearly, it had been swept and mopped over the weekend. I went to the seat where I thought Lord Pentland had been sitting and reached underneath. There was his hat. Evidently, the cleaning crew hadn't taken the time to check under the seats.

Was it a coincidence, a stroke of luck that I'd been in the theatre that night? Had he left the hat on purpose to see if I would be able to get it back?

Both explanations ring false. I felt then, as I did on similar occasions, that I was a minor character in an event that was unfolding according to laws I couldn't understand.

Context

As forbidding as Lord Pentland could appear to some, he could be infinitely kind and gracious to others. He might set what seemed like unreasonable conditions for one person who wanted an appointment to see him, then have me hand-deliver flowers to someone else. It depended on the individual and the context.

For example, there was a man in one of his groups who held a very high position in the uppermost echelon of the financial world. While people were advised to send a message through the Foundation office if they had to miss a group meeting, this man would always call Lord Pentland personally. I would pick up the phone, and the man's secretary would say: "I have So-and-So on the line for Lord Pentland."

Her assumption, because of her employer's position, was that Lord Pentland would take the call. I understood. It was my own assumption, when I placed a call on Lord Pentland's behalf.

And she was correct. Lord Pentland did accept the call, every time, even though he could have asked me to take a message. As someone with experience in the business world, he must have known what it meant for this man to want to deliver his regrets himself. Yet the same act, from someone else, might well have met with a different response.

On the other hand, things could change. A person might suddenly have access to Lord Pentland's inner circle or entrée to a special opportunity—and then, just as suddenly, that access would disappear. I never had the impression that Lord Pentland's shifts were capricious, however. Unpredictable perhaps, from my limited perspective, but purposeful and impeccably-timed.

A Seat on the Plane

Every six weeks or so, Lord Pentland would make a short trip to San Francisco and always invited someone to come with him. After a while, I began to think: "If those other people get to go, why not me?" Extended time in a less formal, more spontaneous setting than a business office—who wouldn't want that?

The next time Lord Pentland began to plan a trip to the West Coast, I asked if I could come. His stare couldn't have been icier. "Why? Don't you have enough work here in New York?"

Later that same day, Lord Pentland came out of his private office with the woman who had come to speak with him. He led her to my desk and draped his arm around her. It was the same gesture he had made that day at the SEG, with a similar quality—to me—of something exaggerated, staged. "Oh Barbara," he drawled, just as he had drawled in the convention center, "I've invited Victoria to come to California with me. Would you mind booking her a seat right next to mine on the plane?"

I had to accept Victoria's effusive gratitude as I made the arrangements. It would have been wrong to taint her experience with jealousy or resentment—especially since, in her eyes, I got to spend so much time with Lord Pentland in New York.

By having me help Victoria, Lord Pentland gave me a gift—an opportunity to transform greed into generosity, competition into kindness. It was a gift far more valuable than simply holding up a mirror to my ambition and lack of appreciation.

I thought he might "reward me" for this special insight with an invitation to accompany him to California at a later date, but he never did.

The List

Soon after I moved to New York, Dianne Edenfield told me that Lord Pentland had given her a list of eligible men at the Foundation—men he recommended, since she was eager to find a partner. Like the date nut bars, that sounded like an excellent idea.

But when I asked Lord Pentland for a similar list, he looked at me in disgust. "You didn't come here to meet men," he said coldly. "You came here for the Work."

On another occasion, however, I asked the question from a different inner state and received a very different response.

We were standing in the open area of the office, near the table where we had lunch. Suddenly everything became very quiet. I felt myself standing there in the silence with Lord Pentland. All at once, I gave voice to the question that had been troubling me so deeply: "I wonder about my future as a woman."

This time, Lord Pentland looked at me with what I can only describe as pure loving-kindness. "You've no idea how beautiful you look right now," he said. Then he told me: "Your 'future as a woman' doesn't depend on having one—or two—men in your bed, but on how many people you can shelter behind your skirts."

Later, he added: "When you're no longer afraid of being alone, you'll want someone who can step on your corns and make your life more difficult."

I had never shared my personal history with Lord Pentland, yet somehow he knew—despite my adventures in places like Turkey, Greece, and Egypt—that I had led a very sheltered, struggle-free life. His observation was uncannily prescient.

As with all of Lord Pentland's remarks, they were specific to the person and the moment. It would be a mistake to take them as universal maxims or apply them indiscriminately to other people, just as it would be a mistake to assume that "behind your skirts" was meant to imply something sexist or pre-feminist. Although Lord Pentland was a prolific writer, often framing his thoughts on a very broad scale, he was also a master of the "oral tradition"—the spoken response, a precise teaching offered at a precise moment.

I remember when several of us were sharing memories after Lord Pentland died. One woman said he had told her that she had to be more like a man. Another woman seemed surprised to hear that. "That's so strange," she said. "He told me that I had to be more like a woman."

The list was for Dianne, not me. As it turned out, she married someone who wasn't on it.

A Good Observaton

There was a weekend when Lord Pentland did not attend our Sunday work at the Firehouse, and I arrived at the office on Monday morning desperate to "confess" what I'd done in his absence.

The "sin" that was weighing on me so heavily was how I'd left the team I was supposed to be leading—literally walked away and joined a different team—because I couldn't bear the assault on my vanity that had taken place.

I had spent Saturday preparing as well as I could, even though I knew nothing about the craft of picture-matting we'd been asked to undertake; nonetheless, I'd been given the task and there was a team to lead. However, when I arrived at the Firehouse, I discovered that someone had been put on the team who was, in fact, an expert.

She simply took over, and everyone deferred to her authority. Her assumption was understandable—and useful, in light of the holiday sale we were working toward—but it was too much for my poor ego. After an excruciating hour, I pushed out my chair, got up, and walked away.

Even as it occurred, my behavior felt entirely counter to the values of the Work. My only hope was in confessing how vanity had triumphed over the openness—or, at the very least, the stoic acceptance—that I felt certain was required.

Lord Pentland listened carefully to my story. Then he said: "Good observation. Keep it up."

His words stunned me. That was it? I'd done something so antithetical to everything Gurdjieff had taught. It couldn't be brushed aside! Without penance and absolution, the sin would remain.

Then his message penetrated. What matters, he was telling me, is the act of observation, not the thing observed.

And, further: if vanity and running away weren't "sins," then endurance wasn't a "virtue"—not in itself, not without seeing.

My behavior at the Firehouse was simply that: behavior. Observed, it might nourish me. Unobserved, it was of no interest.

An Exercise

One time, Lord Pentland related a story about a woman who came to see him and wanted an exercise. He gave her the exercise of taking a cold shower every morning.

According to his story, when she returned the following week, he asked her how the exercise had gone. "Oh, I did it the very next day," she replied, "and it was easy! May I have a new exercise now?"

As with many of Lord Pentland's stories, I had no idea if the incident had really taken place. But it fit with what he had said more than once—the very first time I met him, in fact, at a meeting for brand-new people in Los Angeles.

He had been speaking about the idea of being in prison, and people were responding in what seemed to me, at the advanced age of nineteen, to be a very literal way. I began to say something about how my own feeling of being "in prison" was more internal. Then, feeling too conspicuous, I stopped and said, "Never mind."

Lord Pentland looked right into me. "You give up," he said. "That's one of your features."

Later he told me, "You have to be a warrior." I didn't see myself as timid and helpless, but I was, and it caused many difficulties in life for me.

I can't presume to know Lord Pentland's intention in telling me about the woman who took a single cold shower and then wanted another, more "advanced," exercise. Yet nothing he did was gratuitous.

Slicing the Pizza

Several of us went to Lord Pentland's apartment after the October 29 memorial service for Mr. Gurdjieff, and Lord Pentland ordered a pizza for lunch.

When the pizza arrived, he asked me to cut it. I studied the pizza, trying to sense my arm and decide where to make the perfect intentional cuts that would divide the pie into six exact pieces. After a few moments, Lord Pentland grabbed the knife, exclaiming, "I can't stand it." Whack, whack. He slashed the pizza into six more-or-less equivalent slices, then gave the knife back to me.

On another occasion, Pierre and Vivian Elliott, heirs to the line of Work begun by John G. Bennett, one of Gurdjieff's English pupils, came to see Lord Pentland at his office. It was an important moment—not as important, perhaps, as David Sinker's visit, but a crucial step in opening up a channel of goodwill between Claymont, the center Bennett had established in America, and the Gurdjieff Foundation.

Since their appointment was at eleven o'clock, I asked Pierre and Vivian if they'd like to join Lord Pentland for coffee. They said yes, they would. Then I turned and paused in the doorway to ask if they took cream. "Milk, please," Vivian replied.

Knowing I didn't have any milk and, no doubt, reading the look on my face, Lord Pentland sauntered past me and whispered, "Just add water to the half-and-half."

It was a simple and obvious solution— Lord Pentland's solution, because I was too flustered and slow. I slipped down the hall and got a glass of water to dilute the cream. If Vivian could taste the difference, she didn't let on.

Incidents like these, insignificant as they might sound, carried a profound lesson about responding directly to the moment—being alive, present, instead of trying to be "better" or dreaming about higher states. Lord Pentland offered the lesson with a subtlety that left it up to the listener to spot the message—or not.

On my very first day in the office, for example, Wendy was demonstrating how to organize the incoming mail. I stood behind her, off to the side, as Lord Pentland glanced through an architectural magazine that someone had sent him. "We should subscribe to this some time," he remarked.

The comment drifted right past me—until Wendy pulled me aside and whispered. "He means subscribe to it *now*."

I wasn't quick enough to understand the message in his words, something Wendy had learned in her time working for him.

A Window

One afternoon, a man from the Los Angeles Foundation called to say that he was in New York and hoped Lord Pentland would be able to see him. I remembered the man, since we had been in the same group before I moved to Berkeley, and knew his background of instability. Although he greeted me as if we were old friends, I kept a polite and professional tone, pressed the *hold* button, and related his request to Lord Pentland.

Lord Pentland told me to ask him if he had a job and an apartment. The man said no, he'd just arrived. When I told Lord Pentland, he looked straight at me for a long, penetrating moment. Then he said, "He's no good, is he?"

The air around us was still as Lord Pentland held my gaze. I didn't feel critical and punitive toward the man, nor any desire to be "helpful" and "kind." I knew who he was, knew about events that had transpired a decade earlier, but had no opinion about what was appropriate for him now. I felt entirely neutral, like a window or a mirror, as if Lord Pentland could read the man's entire life, past and future, in my eyes—as if my whole purpose, right then, was to give Lord Pentland access to that vision.

Seconds passed. Then Lord Pentland said: "Tell him I'm away."

The man told me that he was hoping to move to New York and join one of Lord Pentland's groups, but he went back to Los Angeles a few days later. He was never able to hold down a steady job and eventually stopped coming to meetings.

Another Way of Speaking

Early on, I had my heart broken—or so I thought—by a member of one of Lord Pentland's older groups.

I was walking down the street with Lord Pentland, on our way to the Foundation, when the words burst out of me: "I don't want to lose the beautiful happiness I was feeling."

The contradiction in my outburst rang in the autumn air—the inappropriateness of injecting a remark like that into our silent walk, and its truth, which was different from the way I'd been formulating my misery.

"It's not so much the person himself," I found myself adding, "so it makes me wonder if there's something partly false about my suffering."

Lord Pentland's voice was mild. "If the suffering is partly false, it means the happiness was partly false too."

His responses were layered, nuanced, and seldom predictable. One day he would yawn while I was speaking—stretching his mouth in a yawn that seemed to go on forever and making it clear that my statement or question was of no importance. Another day he would turn to me with a huge smile, as if I were his favorite person in the world. He might ask for my opinion—for example, on who ought to join him for a Tuesday evening panel—or look right through me as if I were part of the office furniture.

Once, when I asked if a certain person could be on the kitchen team for our weekend Work, he said: "She hasn't yet demonstrated that she can produce something non-poisonous."

Lord Pentland's declarations were elegant and incisive—koans, buried treasure that took a long time to excavate and required something other than an ordinary, though capable, mind that always tried to "figure out" what he meant.

The Check

We were raising money for a Movements film when a letter arrived for Lord Pentland from a man who had been in one of his groups but had subsequently left the Work. The letter contained a substantial check—an amount the man could easily afford, since he was the head of a successful accounting firm and had, in fact, helped with the Foundation's tax returns. Along with the check was a note expressing his wish to make a contribution to the Work.

Lord Pentland told me to send the check back.

As he later wrote in an essay called *Religion and Money*:

> Like everything existing, money is a vital part of life on the planet and is worthy of respect, of course at its proper level... Without a long work on oneself, it is impossible in contemporary conditions to be generous and free in regard to the force of money. Only those who are truly free understand how to use it as part of the demand they make on others for payment and sacrifice (quoted with permission from *The Gurdjieff International Rev*iew, Vol. IX, No. 1).

When someone who had come to meet with him for the first time announced, with a certain pride, that he didn't care about money, Lord Pentland told him: "How do you know, if you've never had any?"

Five Dollars

One evening, we showed a special film at a place around the corner from the Foundation, known as the Gallery. My task was to stand in the doorway and collect five dollars from each person as they went in.

Lord Pentland was in line, like everyone else. As he drew near, he began to walk past me. I could sense that he wanted to see if I would defer and let him pass, or do my job. My gesture was a beat late. It wasn't until he was about to walk through the door—staring straight ahead, his face expressionless—that I stopped him and said: "Lord Pentland, I need to collect five dollars from you."

He turned to me with a look of innocent surprise. "Oh. Yes, of course." He took out his wallet with excruciating slowness, and the line of people came to a halt behind him. More slowly still, he reached inside and held out a five-dollar bill, but didn't let it go. He made me tug and take it from him.

My Salary

Despite my brash question about salary that day at the San Francisco convention center, I soon discovered how impossible it was to live in New York on the salary Lord Pentland was paying me. Determined to make a convincing case, I drew up a long, detailed list of monthly expenses, with everything from bottles of shampoo to quarters for the laundromat.

Lord Pentland looked at the paper, then handed it back to me. "My dear," he said, "it's all right to do this with me, but don't ever wear your heart on your sleeve like that again." He gave me a raise.

With matters pertaining to the office, in contrast, I *did* have to account for every expenditure. There was a petty cash fund, and Lord Pentland told me that the success of the business depended on keeping track of every single penny. From time to time, I offered to show him my careful tallies, but he always declined.

Sometimes Lord Pentland would write a check for $500 made out to *cash* and ask me to walk to the Bank of New York at Seventy-Third and Madison to cash it for him. I remember walking the six long blocks back to the office—clutching my purse, terrified that I'd lose the money or that someone would know I was carrying what seemed like a fortune.

I had to type my own salary checks and give them to Lord Pentland to sign. I felt like a child waiting for him to approve my weekly allowance. I would stand there every Friday while he examined the check and finally, taking his time, signed his name.

Relationships

Lord Pentland was interested in a wide range of people—interesting people who were doing interesting things—and not just those in the Gurdjieff Work. He had a lively relationship with Kristin Linklater, the Scottish-born voice and acting teacher, as well as with Buddhist scholars, innovators, and avant-garde theater directors, and always gave generously of his time to anyone researching the Sinclair clan. He seemed to especially relish the days when he had appointments with people who were *not* in the Gurdjieff groups.

I can recall the boisterous meetings with Stuart Lyons of Pinewood Studios, the studio outside London that produced the *Meetings with Remarkable Men* film, and Ben Barenholtz of Libra Films, the American distributor. It was fascinating to see Lord Pentland at the head of the conference table, orchestrating the conversation among an eclectic group of Remar personnel, including two attorneys from the Foundation. Lyons called him *Governor*, in acknowledgement of Lord Pentland's peerage, while Barenholtz would take me aside to ask, in clandestine tones, if we had any of "our people" in whatever new city where the film would be opening who could help to promote it.

Lord Pentland also maintained relationships with people who were connected to Gurdjieff's teaching, directly and indirectly—for example, editors at the publishing houses that handled the Gurdjieff books—and others who were interested in Gurdjieff's ideas but weren't part of the Foundation.

One of these was a man named Arkady Rovner, a Russian scholar who came to see Lord Pentland on a number of occasions to ask for assistance in researching Gurdjieff's life. Lord Pentland was gracious, open, and helpful, and Rovner always expressed his deep gratitude. I remember spotting him on the steps of the church after

Lord Pentland's funeral—alone, since he knew none of the people in the Foundation. He had come to mourn, and I went to greet him and thank him for coming, as I knew Lord Pentland would have wanted me to do.

Lord Pentland also managed the complicated relationship between the Foundation and Gurdjieff's heirs—the nieces and nephews, led by Sylvie Anastasieff, wife of Gurdjieff's nephew—who were sure the Foundation was cheating them of their rightful inheritance. Whenever an angry letter arrived from Sylvie, he would greet it with delight, as if knowing that an interesting challenge was in store. "Ah, good!" he would exclaim. "A letter from Sylvie!"

With his red, cloth-bound French-English dictionary close at hand, Lord Pentland would translate the letter aloud as I recorded the English words on my pad. I always had the impression that he enjoyed dealing with someone who was telling him off instead of deferring to him.

A Walk In Central Park

As someone with a keen interest in life, Lord Pentland seemed to have little regard for people who tried to use Foundation activities as a way to fill their otherwise empty hours—as I did, those first weeks in New York.

With no friends to be with on the weekend, I felt lost and alone in an unfamiliar city whose winter landscape—bleak, leafless, and cold—seemed to mirror my inner state. Desperate for something to do and a place to belong, I asked Lord Pentland if I could attend the Sunday of work at Armonk, which was where the groups convened before moving to the Firehouse in Sparkill.

But Lord Pentland refused. "Oh, I'm sure you're too busy settling in," he said.

I spent a long, difficult Sunday walking in Central Park, wandering through the Metropolitan Museum of Art, and trying not to let self-pity overwhelm me. I understood that Lord Pentland wasn't going to let me use Work activities as a cure for my loneliness, but that didn't make it easy.

Later, it was different. The following summer, as he was about to leave for California—literally, on his way out the door—he turned, walked back to my desk, and suggested that I might want to go to the special week at Armonk that was starting the next day.

"Yes, of course," I said. I was already making a frantic mental list of everything I'd have to do to arrange that. It was especially complicated because a younger cousin was arriving that very evening who was planning to stay with me for a few days while she explored Manhattan.

"Call Jim Wyckoff," Lord Pentland added, "and let him know you're coming."

Jim Wyckoff was one of the senior people at the Foundation who would be leading the Work period. He seemed taken aback by my call, and I was too wrapped up in my own list of tasks to realize that being a last-minute addition would create difficulty for the Armonk planners who didn't know me and now had to arrange a ride, a bed, and a place on a team.

The day after the week at Armonk ended, I flew to California for a period of Work in San Francisco with Lord Pentland. I wouldn't have minded an afternoon to stroll through Central Park or a museum, but there wasn't time.

The Telegram

Late one Saturday evening, the phone rang in my apartment. It was Lord Pentland, calling from San Francisco. Kathryn Hulme, author of *Undiscovered Country* and one of the women who had worked closely with Gurdjieff in the 1940s, had just died. "Can you take down a telegram?" he asked.

I scrambled for a pad and pen as Lord Pentland began to dictate what turned out to be an exceptionally long message. When he was finished, he said, "Call Western Union and have them send it to Madame de Salzmann in Paris."

I did as he asked, but later began to wonder why he hadn't called Western Union himself. Wouldn't that have been more "efficient" than dictating a message that I would just have to repeat to someone else?

When I mentioned that to Lois Bry, who had been the secretary of the Gurdjieff Foundation for many years, she smiled. "He doesn't care about efficiency," she said. "He was giving you an opportunity to work."

Her words were like a bell. Of course she was right. The longer path—the detour to include another person—provided an exchange, an experience. And, strange as the idea seemed, perhaps it helped Lord Pentland too. Dictating the message to me, even with my imperfect attention, might have allowed him to work out what to say in a way that wouldn't have been possible if he'd been talking to a Western Union clerk.

Lois Bry's remark opened a new thought—the possibility that we are all needed, at moments and in ways we might never know.

The New Room

Space at the Foundation was always at a premium, with a limited number of rooms and an increasingly complex schedule of groups and meetings. Then Lord Pentland had an inspiration for where an additional room could be built—above, in the two-stories-high space of the large upstairs room known as the Studio.

I don't recall if it was Dick Brower or Jon Rothenberg, Lord Pentland's son-in-law, who related the story, but apparently Lord Pentland had looked up one evening, in the middle of a group meeting, and realized that there was an entire "room" of unused space overhead. He put Jon in charge of construction, and before long there was an additional meeting room and a brand-new staircase.

After a bit of time had passed, Dick brought up the room at one of our office lunches. "Isn't it time to give it a permanent name?" he asked Lord Pentland. After all, the other rooms had names, like the Apartment or the Crow's Nest. Dick had prepared a list of suggestions.

But Lord Pentland merely raised a distinctive eyebrow. "Why?" he asked. "It's still called the New Testament."

That was in 1983. It remains The New Room.

Jumping Mouse

One unforgettable experience was the play at the Firehouse that the four of us living in the Loft had to prepare on a week's notice. The Loft was a former industrial space in a building near Astor Place that was used for a variety of purposes, from craft work to events for new people to an experiment in communal living, all under Lord Pentland's direction. Bruce and I, recently married, were living there with two women from our group at the Foundation.

Just as we were ending a Sunday of work at the Firehouse, Lord Pentland took me aside and said, "I thought perhaps the Loft could put on a little play next Sunday, at the end of the day. A suitable story, costumes, that sort of thing."

As always, the answer was *yes, of course.* But the task was daunting. The only one of us who knew anything about putting on a play was Bruce, a former actor. As it happened, though, he was going out of town on a business trip and wouldn't be back until Friday night. We had to get everything together—find "a suitable story," turn it into a script, memorize our lines, create costumes—with only a single day, Saturday, to rehearse.

This was long before people could send documents by email. Instead, I made a Xerox copy of the story we had found—a Native American tale called *The Story of Jumping Mouse*—and sent it to Bruce by overnight mail so he could study it in his hotel room and think about how to stage it.

Somehow, we got everything ready by the following Sunday. Then, just as the play was about to begin, with eighty people waiting eagerly in their chairs, Lord Pentland beckoned to us. "Perhaps you could add one more thing?" he said. "While you're playing your parts, maybe you could each imitate one of the group leaders."

When the four of us talked about the experience, later, we all agreed: by getting the play ready in six short days, we had already accomplished the seemingly-impossible, so the actual performance was unimportant—unless Lord Pentland made it impossible again. And he did that in a way that required something completely different from the determined focus that had gotten us through the week. He asked us to risk everything we had planned and rehearsed—to draw on our observations, but without caricature, and dare to be free and spontaneous.

I remember catching a glimpse of Dick Brower, the person I had decided to imitate, and seeing the confusion on his face as he saw *something*, but didn't know what it was and didn't understand why people were laughing.

The Sale

The annual Christmas sale at the Firehouse was an event that required months of preparation. In addition to producing an inventory of hand-crafted items, we had to transform the building itself—from the display window out front, which always featured an animated winter scene, to the wreaths and holiday decorations that turned a bare, neutral space into a center of festivity.

The sale was the way we raised the money needed to keep the place going. It was also the time when we interfaced with the public, since the event was open to friends, family, and the Sparkill community. There was a café, a children's area with Santa and presents, and entertainment provided by dancers and musicians in Lord Pentland's groups. The focus, however, was on the crafts that were for sale.

One year, Lord Pentland asked several of us to oversee the creation of elaborate booths where the items would be displayed. The design and construction of the booths was a long and complicated effort, capping months of work on the products themselves. Then, right before the doors opened, Lord Pentland gathered the four of us who were in charge of the booths—the same way he had gathered the foursome who lived at the Loft just before the play began.

This time, he suggested that we compete with one another to see who could bring in the most money. That might, he added, include trying to steal each other's customers through whatever maneuvers we could devise.

At first, I found the suggestion appalling. Yet we all plunged in, and a spirit of playful merriment began to spread through the Firehouse—better suited to a Christmas sale, in fact, than our solemn "work faces" had been. We did, indeed, try to cajole, trick, bribe, and seduce each other's customers. The guests seemed to enjoy our antics, and perhaps that was the impression Lord Pentland wanted them to have—that we were light and open, rather than stiff and serious.

I couldn't help remembering the difficulties the San Francisco group had experienced with their neighbors. The St. Elmo property was in an exclusive residential part of the city, and the nearby homeowners resented the cars, construction, and Sunday activity that marred the refined ambiance. Sparkill offered a chance to do things differently.

Those musings didn't occur to me until after the sale. While I was trying to woo Henry Jacobson away from John Sullivan's booth, I was simply having a good time.

A Restaurant In Tribeca

A member of one of Lord Pentland's groups had just opened what later became a "culinary landmark" in TriBeCa, long before the neighborhood became trendy. The restaurant was a family project among the three brothers and their mother, all of whom were deeply invested in its success, both financially and emotionally.

Lord Pentland decided that we would hold our January 13 celebration there, right in the middle of an industrial section of Manhattan that no one had heard of or knew how to find, instead of at the Foundation where it was traditionally held. Sam, the group member who was part-owner, had to convince his brothers, who were not in the Work, to let us take over the place for an evening. The only way we were permitted to do that, after much negotiating, was on the strict condition that we do no cooking on-site and leave everything exactly as we had found it. Sam's eldest brother, resistant and suspicious, was adamant that we couldn't use any of his kitchen equipment, other than warming up a few trays in the oven.

The evening created an unforgettable demand. We had to photograph every inch of the kitchen and dining room to be sure that we restored everything to its place, and wrap enormous pans of food—cooked at the Loft—in blankets and down coats before whisking them into taxis.

Certainly, the event could have been held in an easier, "more logical" location whose atmosphere was conducive to commemorating Gurdjieff. But this way, we had to create our own atmosphere—from nothing except our own work.

The question of an atmosphere was one that Lord Pentland often returned to. When someone asked him why he had started the experiment in communal living at the Loft, he said that he was interested in what it might be to establish an atmosphere.

It was an elusive question. While he gave us special unpublished readings and sent interesting guests our way, we still had to deal with each other—negotiating chores, expenses, and personalities, and sharing a single bathroom. Whatever atmosphere might appear, at times, came from our wish to meet the conditions he had offered.

Washington Square

Lord Pentland gave a number of public talks during the years I worked for him. One of the first that I recall was at New York University in 1980.

The talk was arranged by Ann Fremantle, widow of Lord Pentland's close friend Christopher Fremantle. Ann was friendly with NYU Professor of Religion James Carse and was eager to bring the two men together. On her introduction, Lord Pentland agreed to give a lecture on Gurdjieff for Carse's undergraduate class. My impression was that he was intrigued by the challenge of conveying the flavor of Gurdjieff's teaching to young people who knew nothing about it.

On the day of the talk, Lord Pentland asked me to meet him at NYU. We were traveling separately, since he was coming from his apartment and I had to leave from the office with a box of books, copies of the newly-published *Toward Awakening* that he wanted me to sell to the students, or try to. Shortly before I left, however, the phone rang. It was Professor Carse, letting us know that the location of the class had been switched to a different building. I tried to call Lord Pentland at his apartment, but he didn't answer.

I headed to the revised location at NYU. The students were already there, waiting. I needed to find Lord Pentland—quickly. In an era of cell phones and text messages, the situation may be hard to fathom. But back then, there was no way to get a message to someone who wasn't near a landline.

Something drew me to the window. I looked down at Washington Square—the arch and fountain, the crowd of students thronging in all directions. Suddenly, there was the tall, straight, unmistakable figure of Lord Pentland striding rapidly along a diagonal path. It was as if my awareness telescoped back to the moment in San Francisco when I saw him in the middle of a crowded geophysical convention. My purpose was clear: to find Lord Pentland, in the midst of life.

I ran down the four flights of stairs, out the door, and straight to the spot where my intuition said he would be, given his pace and the angle of the path. "Lord Pentland!" I shouted.

He turned around—surprised to see me, or pretending to be. I told him where the class was meeting, and he accompanied me back to the building.

Wagner College

Another talk took place at Wagner College in Staten Island, in 1983. This event came about through the persistence of a member of the Edgar Cayce Foundation who was organizing a seminar on "Parallel Paths to Self-Discovery" and wanted to highlight the similarities and differences between Cayce's teachings, *A Course in Miracles*, and the Gurdjieff Work. Although he initially declined, Lord Pentland eventually agreed to take part.

A week or two before the seminar, someone from the Cayce Foundation called the office asking for a photo of Lord Pentland for the brochure. Since Lord Pentland had no "official" photo—in general, there are few pictures of him—he asked me to call David Sailors, a member of the group who was a professional photographer.

When David arrived at the office with his camera, Lord Pentland faced him and told him to go ahead. David readied the camera and took a picture. Lord Pentland turned, went into his office, and closed the door. One chance, one photo.

On the day of the conference, six of us accompanied Lord Pentland to Wagner College: Mary and Jon Rothenberg, Loraine and Joel Voros, Bruce and me. Between the morning and afternoon sessions, we were joined for lunch by the woman from the Cayce Foundation who had arranged the program.

I remember how she looked around the table at us and remarked, "You're like a family." There was something puzzled and wistful in her voice.

The Doorman

There was no hiding anything from Lord Pentland, whether it was the chocolate I'd taken from the round little tin in his office and stuffed in the drawer, half-eaten, when he returned earlier than expected—or a moment's lapse of conscience.

Lord Pentland had invited me to attend the special Friday evening sittings for the oldest members of the Foundation while Madame de Salzmann was in town. The sittings were by invitation only, and the doorman checked the names against a list. A single moment of forgetting cost me that privilege.

It was late on a Friday, well after five o'clock, but Lord Pentland was still in the office. I was at my desk, far enough away that he might not have heard—if I hadn't raised my voice, half showing-off and half flirting with the person on the phone.

The caller was one of the attorneys Lord Pentland counted on for advice about Foundation matters, a charming and attractive man who had always treated me warmly. I relayed the message that Lord Pentland had asked me to give him, then sang out merrily, in loud and affected French, "See you later. *A six heures et demie!*"

I felt Lord Pentland's antennae go up, the same way they had that day in the library in San Francisco, and I knew. He didn't say a word, but when I arrived at the Foundation for the special six-thirty sitting, the doorman stopped me. "I'm sorry," he said, "but you're not on the list. Lord Pentland removed your name."

Lord Pentland's lesson, and his gift—though a message delivered by a poker-faced doorman—was the sensation of a profound inner contradiction. Two contradictory forces—angel and devil, equally matched—created a moment of self-awareness that the angel alone could never have brought about.

I still remember that moment in the Foundation lobby, as I took in the doorman's words, although I don't remember what Madame de Salzmann said in the sittings that I did attend.

An Event At The Barbizon Hotel

The New York Foundation was less than a block from the Barbizon Hotel, a landmark building that served for decades as a residential hotel for women. The hotel had an oversized pool where many of us would go to swim during the hour before our group meetings.

Ironically, the Barbizon was also where the most aggressive "pseudo-Gurdjieff group" held its events. We called them "the bookmark people" because they inserted their bookmarks, with colorful advertisements for their gatherings, into Gurdjieff's and Ouspensky's books at the esoteric bookstores in New York like Samuel Weiser's and Quest. We even had a special team, headed by Dick Brower, whose task it was to go into the bookstores each week and remove the bookmarks.

Lord Pentland sent me to attend one of their introductory events. As it happened, the event was at the same time as my group meeting, which I would now be missing. "See what you can observe," Lord Pentland said, "and tell me about it tomorrow."

Aware that my "real" Gurdjieff group was convening only a block away, I set out for the Barbizon. I followed the signs to the correct room and took a seat facing the stage. There was a panel presentation, followed by coffee and conversation. During the coffee hour, we were asked to mingle with members of the organization while refraining from using the word *I*. I remember thinking that it was a silly exercise, obvious and artificial, but I did it anyway. In fact, it was quite difficult. Later, when I went to write up my observations, I was surprised by how much I recalled.

The next morning, Lord Pentland asked how the evening had gone. I began to relate what had taken place, the criticism in my voice all-too-apparent, but he cut me off. "You should be glad and wish for anyone who's trying to benefit from what Gurdjieff brought," he said.

Then I described my experience with the exercise of not using the word *I*. Again, an undercurrent of scorn slipped into my voice. Lord Pentland stopped me a second time.

"They helped you," he said. "You ought to thank them."

A Mistake

On another occasion, I went to Lord Pentland's apartment with the galleys of a long article that Margaret Croyden had written for the *New York Times Magazine* about the *Meetings with Remarkable Men* film, which was about to open. Getting the piece, with full-color photographs, into the Sunday *Magazine* was a significant coup. I knew Lord Pentland wanted to have an early look and brought the galleys to him as soon as they arrived.

I was horrified to discover, however, after my diligent proofreading, that there was a small mistake. "Why is it always like that?" I asked him.

"It's no one's fault," he replied. "It's just our level of being."

Blind

We were having a crafts sale at the Gallery, around the corner from the Foundation and were encouraged to invite friends and family. I invited my sister, who was living in Brooklyn, since I was curious for her to meet Lord Pentland.

Many people have stories about meeting Lord Pentland for the first time and knowing, at once, that he was unlike anyone they had ever encountered—as if the vibration of his being cut right through their images and expectations, and they felt *seen* in a way they had never experienced.

My sister, on the other hand, had no expectation, no interest in esoteric ideas or spiritual development. All I said, when I introduced them, was that he was my employer.

Lord Pentland looked at her, into her, for a long moment. Later, I asked her what she thought of him. She said, "He's blind, isn't he?"

When I asked why she thought that, she told me, "There wasn't anything in his eyes when he looked at me, so I figured he must be blind."

Her conclusion was striking for its unintentional precision: if one can't receive the experience of being seen, it will be taken for its opposite.

The Accountant

Though not everyone saw this side of him, Lord Pentland was one of the funniest people I've ever met. He had a dry wit and a perfectly-honed sense of timing. His face would light up at the absurdities that came his way—like the lavish card that arrived in the mail one day, announcing that our accounting firm was changing its name from *Bohrer, Bohrer, Rosenfarb and Licata* (a name Lord Pentland found hilarious) to *Bohrer, Rosenfarb and Licata.*

He seemed to have great fun with the accountant, to whom he always appeared as a confused, daffy, somewhat senile English eccentric. The accountant would take me aside and whisper, "See if you can get Lord Pentland to sign these papers without messing them up this time."

On A Street Corner

As mentioned, whenever *Meetings with Remarkable Men* was going to open in a city where there was a Gurdjieff group, we made arrangements to ship posters and flyers so group members could help with promotion.

By chance, I was going to be in Providence, Rhode Island, when the film would be shown there. I didn't know if there was a group in Providence—in fact, there wasn't—but Lord Pentland told me to get in touch with a man whose name I didn't recognize. I called the man, who agreed to take some posters and asked me to meet him on a particular street corner.

Forty years later, the meeting remains as vivid as the day it happened. I was walking down the sidewalk on an ordinary inner-city street, heading to the corner where we had agreed to meet. Up ahead, at the end of the block, there was a cyclone fence surrounding a basketball court where a half-dozen black teenagers were shooting baskets with a middle-aged white man. As I neared the court, an extraordinary energy began to fill me, growing stronger and more palpable with each step. The man saw me approaching, handed the basketball to one of the boys, and came to the sidewalk to greet me.

It was clear that the energy was radiating from the man himself. I gave him the posters. He thanked me and returned to the court where the teenagers were waiting.

I never saw the man again, nor did Lord Pentland ever mention his name. Yet the impression was imprinted on me of a man working in life, hidden in plain sight. The experience was another of Lord Pentland's gifts.

The Ending
February 1984

Lord Pentland's last hours in the office were on Monday morning, February 13, 1984. He had a luncheon planned with someone visiting from the West Coast and several afternoon appointments, but he went home early.

"I'm going back to the apartment," he said. "I'm not feeling very well." He asked me to call the people he was supposed to see and extend his apologies.

I had a fleeting sensation—like a glimpse through a door, as it was shutting—that there was something odd about what he had said, something I should stop and notice, because Lord Pentland never spoke about his, or anyone's, health. Even when I'd had a bad cold and spent the day wheezing and coughing, he never commented on it, as if giving my sneezes any attention would elevate them to an unnecessary importance.

His remark should have alerted me to the gravity of the moment, but it didn't. In my Barbara-efficient way, I shifted my attention to the Rolodex so I could find the phone numbers of the people to call. When I looked up again, he was gone.

If I'd had the presence to realize that something important was happening—if I'd heeded that sound of a distant bell—what would I have done? Marked the moment, taken it in more fully, grabbed a final "significant" memory to treasure?

Perhaps it could have gone no other way. I acted according to my nature, and am left with the indelible impression of how seldom my subconscious mind connects with my conscious mind.

I arrived at the office a little before nine o'clock the next morning—Tuesday, February 14. As was my pattern, I went into Lord Pentland's private office to turn on the desk lamp and wind the clock. I had just begun to set up the coffee maker when the phone rang. I was sure it was Lord Pentland, because no one else ever called at 8:58. Instead, it was Dick Brower, telling me that Lord Pentland had died a few hours earlier.

I couldn't believe what he was telling me, as if there was no context in which *Lord Pentland died* could make sense. Then I took it in, and said yes, I would call the Foundation and make the other necessary calls. I stood by my desk for a long moment and then, slowly, walked into Lord Pentland's office and turned off the lamp.

As the day progressed, people began to gather at the apartment of Lord Pentland's daughter Mary, who lived in the same building. Her apartment became the center of activity, and Dick went there too. Yet I felt, foolishly or not, that I had to stay and keep the office open—that it was my task, my place; that people deserved to have a real person answer the phone and not a machine; and that it was what Lord Pentland would have wanted me to do.

In fact, no one called. The news had been circulated through the group secretaries, and there was no reason for anyone to call Lord Pentland's private office. Business was quiet that day as well, as if it too had stopped.

If I had to conclude with a single statement about Lord Pentland as I knew him in his "regular" life, it would be that he was always working and always teaching. From my line of sight, limited as it may have been, there was no separation between the two: his work was for himself and for others, and his teaching was for himself and for others.

As I reflect on my time with him, I see that he taught me in ways that were both direct and indirect—direct because they were right there, alive in the moment, yet indirect because they were often in the form of hints or seeds that only came to fruition much later.

His wish for us, I believe, was that we have both the opportunity and the courage to *go beyond*. I will never forget when Michael Currer-Briggs—an older man from the London group who had spent time in New York to help with promotion of *Meetings with Remarkable Men*—wrote me a letter from London in which he begged the "elders" in the Foundation to allow younger people to step forward and take responsibility. Lord Pentland felt so strongly about the letter that he had me attend the next Group One meeting and read it aloud to the assembled "elders." The future of the Work, he seemed to imply, depended on providing for those who would come next. Whether that task has been carried out remains to be seen.

In our time together, Lord Pentland never taught by lecturing or correcting me, nor would he give obvious answers. Instead, he placed me squarely in front of myself.

What more could I have possibly wanted?

ACKNOWLEDGEMENTS

Gratitude to David Appelbaum for his keen editorial eye and support of this project, and to early readers Bruce Probst and Loraine Corfield for their valuable insights. Special thanks, as well, to Luis Morales for his skill in bringing new life to forty-year-old photos.

Remembrance to those who were part of these years, named and unnamed in this manuscript, but are no longer with us.

ABOUT THE AUTHOR

Barbara Probst is a writer of fiction and nonfiction living on an historic dirt road in the lower Hudson Valley. Her previous work includes a book for parents of out-of-the-box children, a textbook on clinical assessment and diagnosis, and two award-winning novels, published as Barbara Linn Probst; a third novel will release in October 2022.

Barbara served as Lord Pentland's secretary from November 1978 until his death in February 1984. She holds a PhD in clinical social work from Fordham University.